THE IRON, STEEL AND COAL INDUSTRY IN NORTH STAFFORDSHIRE

A Brief Account

By

Allan C. Baker

As in most industrialised parts of the country, canals preceded railways, so it is fitting that we should start our exploration with a canal scene. This is the Trent and Mersey Canal at Stoke, showing to the extreme left its junction with the Newcastle-under-Lyme Canal: the view looks north in 1967. The Trent and Mersey Canal was our first man-made waterway on a national scale, hence its original title The Grand Trunk, running 93⅜ miles from Preston Brook near Middlewich where it connects with the Bridgewater Canal, to Derwent Mouth near Derby, where it joins the River Trent. It opened throughout in 1777. The Newcastle-under-Lyme Canal ran four miles to the town of that name, and opened sometime in 1800. Closed as a through route in 1921, a remaining section as far as Trent Vale followed in 1935, but a stub remained at the Stoke end, as seen here, to serve as a wharf and mooring. (Map 8) Photograph Allan C. Baker.

This locomotive is one built by Manning Wardle of Leeds, No 1929 of 1917 vintage, originally for the RAF at Cranwell, and seen here in April 1966 whilst working at Parkhouse Colliery, near Chesterton in Newcastle. It is actually standing on the former NSR Chesterton Branch, with the main A34 Trunk Road at a higher level behind. The connection to the colliery sidings left the branch under the bridge taking the road over the railway, the colliery being situated on the other side of the road. BLYTHE No 1, came from Foxfield Colliery near Cheadle, south of the Potteries in September 1965, after that pit closed - hence its name, after a river near there. Stranding alongside is the late Jack Riley, its driver, and a great friend of mine over many years. Jack taught me a lot about industrial railways and locomotives, having earlier worked at both the Apedale colliery and ironworks complex and the Shelton Iron & Steel Works, as well as for a number of years between the wars, on the Kent Coalfield. On the footplate is his Shunter, 'Ligah', I never did know his full name The locomotive was scrapped in January 1969, after the pit itself closed in June the previous year. (Map 4) (Allan C Baker)

Fenton Colliery seen here in the latter part of the 19th century. This pit dates from 1850, and was situated almost in the centre of Fenton itself, the town Arnold Bennett missed out when he 'dubbed' the locality 'The Five Towns', when if one counts Fenton there are six! The upcast shaft is nearest the camera, and notice the smoke emerging from the shaft chimney, indicating an underground furnace to provide draught for ventilation purposes - a practice becoming rare by the time this picture was taken. Always known locally in later days as Glebe Colliery after its one time owners, the pit survived to be vested into the NCB, and did not close until October 1964. In 1947, the saleable output amounted to some 172 217 tons. Note the narrow gauge tubs alongside the heard sticks. (Map 8) (Authors Collection)

ISBN 1-903266-35-1

Dedication

My late Father and Best Friend:
Stephen Allan Baker.
He would have loved to see this book.

Front cover. One of my favourite photographs, used before but one I could not resist using again. Here is Heath's No.15, built at Black Bull in 1915, just breasting the summit of the climb from Birchenwood en-route to Black Bull with returning empties. Notice the wisp at the safety valves, and the tight front end! The dirt tip in the background is Birchenwood, the village behind the train Newchapel, and that on the skyline to the right, Harriseahead. The train is about to pass under the road connecting these two villages. Originally built to bring Birchenwood coke to the Biddulph Valley for the Black Bull and Ford Green Ironworks, latterly the line was used to take Biddulph Valley coal to Birchenwood for coking, and onward transport. (Map 2) Photograph the late Dr. J.R. Hollick.

Back cover. Completely detached from the Potteries coalfield is the Cheadle coalfield, a few miles south-east and working the same coal seams, which outcrop in the intervening area. Coal mining in the Cheadle coalfield goes back many years, and there were numerous small winnings, but only a handful with much in the way of mechanisation. One such was Foxfield Colliery at Dilhorne, north west of the market town of Cheadle and dating from about 1880 when the two shafts, 752ft deep, were sunk. Connection was made with the NSR Derby and Burton-on-Trent line at Blythe Bridge by a three and a half mile long private railway, which opened in 1893. By the following year the pit employed some 130 men, and by 1931 raised 104,643 tons of coal, increasing to 168,615 tons by 1945. This view shows the screens and sidings some time just before the First World War, with the upcast shaft to the left and the downcast to the right. (Map 10)

First published in the
United Kingdom in 2003
by Irwell Press Ltd.,
59A, High Street, Clophill,
Bedfordshire MK45 4BE
Printed by Jetspeed

Foreword

Compilation of this slim volume goes some way to fulfilling a life-long ambition of placing on record, photographically, something of the heavy industry of my native North Staffordshire. Actually the book's coverage is narrower than this, being almost exclusively confined to the six towns and sixty villages that form the conurbation of the City of Stoke-on-Trent, and the adjoining loyal and ancient Borough of Newcastle-under-Lyme. This part of the world is of course famous, then and now, for its pottery and chinaware, a flourishing pottery manufacturing industry growing up amid the abundance of suitable clay and the coal to fire the pottery kilns. As ironstone was found in the explorations for coal, it was natural that an iron and later steel industry grew in the locality too. Other heavy and light engineering was a natural corollary to this.

My interest in the industrial archaeology of North Staffordshire knows no bounds, and largely developed out of a lifetime's fascination with railways, and seeing from the lineside and on family car journeys, those fussy little locomotives that 'messed' around colliery yards and the like. These engines were often painted in bright colours, had names rather than numbers and more importantly did not appear in my ABCs! I very soon learnt however, of the existence of the Birmingham Locomotive Club, and its Industrial Locomotive Information Section – what a mouthful. Members specialised in the study of 'industrial' locomotives as they were known and the 'I.L.I.S.' later became the Industrial Railway Society – the I.R.S. In addition I also discovered the kindred Industrial Locomotive Society, and I have remained a staunch supporter of both bodies ever since. Indeed, to some extent this book is a photographic supplement to the *Industrial Locomotives of North Staffordshire* which I compiled on behalf of the IRS and published in 1997, the result of almost forty years research by myself – let alone the work of those who had gone before me. That book, despite its somewhat narrow title is much more, as it attempts to briefly describe the history and activities of all companies and other undertakings that have owned industrial locomotives, or operated industrial railways, in North Staffordshire. Of course, photographically it confines itself to locomotives, and while I have included a small number of locomotives in this volume, the object has been to illustrate the establishments and environment in which they worked.

By the use of extended captions I have also attempted to give some history of the various undertakings, as well as describing what the photographs actually show. I make no apology on at least two counts however, first for the far from complete coverage of the selected domain. I have confined myself to a very personal collection of photographs, to no small extent dependent to what is available, as there are many other locations I would have wanted to illustrate had photographs been available. In

Plateways, and other early primitive forms of railway, largely came about to act as canal feeders. This rather indistinct photograph, the quality of which I apologise for, is nevertheless worthy of inclusion as it shows the remains of one of the earliest of such plateways, the Lane End (Longton) Tramway. This was the longest of several such lines built to augment the Trent and Mersey Canal, at 2¾ miles long, running from the canal at Whieldon Road Stoke to Lane End south-east of Longton. It was authorised by Act of Parliament in May 1776 and appears to have opened only a short time after the canal itself. Largely passing out of use in about 1850, it followed the course of the main road through Fenton to Longton, and the section seen here is part of what remained for a few more years to serve Fenton Park Colliery. This in turn appears to have fallen out of use in 1895 on closure of the pit there. The view looks down towards the wharf at Whieldon Road from the present Stoke to Fenton and Longton road, formerly the A50, immediately on the Fenton side where it passes over the Stoke to Biddulph and Leek railway line at Pratts Sidings. (Map 8)

Above and overleaf. James Brindley, the well-known early engineer, pioneered the building of the Trent and Mersey Canal and also surveyed the Caldon Canal, which eventually ran 17½ miles from a junction with the Trent and Mersey on its summit at Etruria, to Froghall in the Churnet Valley. It thus served as a feeder to the main line, provided it with much of its water and gave access to the limestone quarries at Caldon Low, between Leek and Ashbourne. It opened in 1779. This and the next photograph shows the railway wagon tippler at Endon, on the Caldon Canal, which enabled main line railway wagons to discharge their loads into canal boats. Coming into use in 1917, it was built in the NSR works at Stoke to the designs of one of the Railway's promising young draughtsman, Thomas F. Coleman, himself a native of Endon, and later to achieve fame as William Stanier's principal locomotive designer. The purpose of the lift was to transfer limestone from the Caldon Quarries to canal boats, for onward transit by canal to the Brunner Mond chemical works at Northwich. Originally this traffic used to travel from the quarries by a succession of rope and gravity tramways from Caldon Low to Froghall, to be transhipped to canal boat there. The North Staffordshire Railway opened a direct line from Leek Brook to the quarries on 1 July 1905 – the Leek, Caldon Low & Hartington Light Railway. At Brunner Mond, however, they preferred the limestone to arrive by canal, so this transhipment arrangement came into existence, saving the traverse of the most torturous section of the Caldon Canal. Although the contract to serve Brunner Mond terminated in 1921, the lift appears to have remained in use until about 1928, presumably for other traffic – it was dismantled soon after. (Map 8) Photographs Collection late Dr J.R. Hollick.

addressing my own favourites, so to speak, I have nevertheless tried to give a reasonable coverage, and the book starts at the north of the area and moves south. Secondly, I make no apology for the condition of some of the prints, the originals often leave a lot to be desired, but are the best it has been possible to collect. This book therefore, is very much an Allan Baker book about North Staffordshire industry, rather than a book about North Staffordshire industry by Allan Baker! Moreover, I do feel the historical importance of what the photographs display, outweighs any deficiencies in their quality.

I have written before how the comparatively small enclave of industrial activity in North Staffordshire, and indeed the Potteries and surrounding villages themselves, forms a distinct centre very much of its own. The locality owes no ties with the rest of the county, or indeed the surrounding counties that border it, Shropshire, Cheshire and Derbyshire, in any way, shape or form. It is very

much 'on its own', and despite the almost total ellipse of heavy industry in recent times, it retains its distinctive individuality. The last deep coal mine closed in December 1998 and the remaining remnants of the once extensive Shelton Iron & Steel Works in April 2000. I left the area well over 25 years ago, but my love of it remains, and if anything is stronger than ever. Despite enormous changes from how I knew it in my childhood, and subsequently, I still derive great satisfaction on my occasional trips 'home'. As I have found out in my subsequent almost nomadic existence, its people are so wonderfully friendly, and I am always proud to tell folk that I am a 'Potter born and bred'.

Over the years hundreds of people, family, friends, colleagues and other acquaintances have helped me in my abounding quest for information. This has ranged from the odd snippet from employees and ex-employees of the industries, who I have been able to locate or search out, talking about events years ago, to the use of Record

Offices, Libraries and the like. To list them all in a book of this size would make it almost twice as long, so I shall have to confine myself to but a few! This is unfortunate, because I so much like penning acknowledgements, and recalling how acquaintances and friendships came about and what was discovered as a result. But it should not be forgotten that not infrequently, the most minor and at the time seemingly insignificant piece of information would later lead to further research, discoveries, and sometimes a mine of other information!

First and foremost I must mention my late Father, who unfortunately will not be able to see this work, but I have nevertheless dedicated it to him. Dad came to North Staffordshire in 1933 at the age of 22, and being enamoured of railways and indeed anything to do with engineering, took a great interest in what was going on around him. Coming as he did from the Fenlands, and despite having served an engineering apprenticeship, the 'Grim Smile of the Five Towns' (apologies to

Arnold Bennett), presented an awesome sight to a young 22 year old with its belching chimneys, colliery dirt tips, iron and steel works and the like; indeed, smoke and grime almost everywhere. As a young Policeman he made it his business when visiting industrial establishments, as he frequently had to, to poke around the engine and boiler rooms, locomotive sheds and the rest, and get to know those in charge of the machinery. Later when driving the Ambulances (in those days manning the Ambulance Service fell to the Police Force) and Police cars, he became very well acquainted with the area and knew it intimately. And as a very accomplished model engineer, eventually with numerous live steam working miniature steam locomotives to his credit, it was but natural that I should become as enthusiastic as he was! And a career as a railway engineer myself – now in `its fortieth year – has set the seal on it.

So I have to thank Dad for introducing me to a lifelong involvement, both professionally and in almost all my spare time, and I do not see it diminishing as I reach retirement. Indeed, it will be the reverse I hope, with more spare time allowing me to delve even deeper into the industrial history of my beloved North Staffordshire. Dad was at Sneyd Colliery with the Ambulance, on that fateful New Years Day in 1942, when no less than 57 men lost their lives in a terrific underground explosion; not a sole who was in the Banbury workings that morning – where the explosion took place – lived to tell the tale. There were other fatal accidents too that Dad

saw at first-hand, so that his 'feeling' for the locality and the people became perhaps greater than that for his native Huntingdonshire. Thanks Dad for everything, and not forgetting the tremendous support we both got from my Mother too.

My friend and mentor in all matters North Staffordshire, for over 25 years, was the late Dr JR (Jack) Hollick, originally from Ashbourne but latterly Hartington. Jack of course, is famous among railway enthusiasts for his pioneering work as a member of the five man 'Manifold' team; they're much sought-after *The North Staffordshire Railway* appearing in 1952. His knowledge of the area, its railways, industries and people was formidable, and I am forever grateful to Jack for his help, assistance and wise council over such a long period. He befriended me from an early age, was generous with his knowledge and extensive collection, when I had nothing to offer in return. Anybody with an interest in this wonderful part of our country is the poorer since Jack's death. Photographs credited to Jack are reproduced by courtesy of the Foxfield Light Railway Society, as Jack left his collection to this local Society. The collection is housed in the Horace Barks Reference Library at Hanley, and permission from the Society is necessary to obtain copies.

Similarly, Bill Jack was very supportive of my interest in the North Staffordshire Coalfield, of which he has an extensive and detailed knowledge. Indeed I doubt anybody would contradict me if I were to say that Bill is the leading authority alive today on

the subject. For many years he was employed at the Chatterley Whitfield Colliery, as were his Father and Uncle, and it is no word of a lie to say that his knowledge of that undertaking is encyclopaedic. Bill has, over as many years as I care to remember, helped me better understand the coal mining industry in the locality, and from all aspects, and in all its vicissitudes.

Others who have helped me include in particular Roger Hateley for his excellent cartography skills; his maps that appear here derive from those he did for *Industrial Locomotives of North Staffordshire*, mentioned earlier. I am grateful to both Roger and the IRS for allowing use of these excellent maps again, suitably amended. Basil Jeuda has once again come to my assistance, as we continue to help each other in our respective research and writings on North Staffordshire. Other helpers have been the late Dave Diable, Dave Donkin, Clive Guthrie, Bernard Holland, the late Jim Peden, Malcolm Rigby, and Tim Shuttleworth, the latter not only for the use of some of his photographs, but also for his excellent work in printing often lousy negatives, or copying battered and dog-eared prints. Of course, I must also thank the other photographers whose work I have used, as well as others whose collections I have borrowed prints from. Particular mention needs to be made of the Keele University Library, where among other gems, the collection of the late EJD Warrillow is kept. Ernest Warrillow was a photographer with the local newspaper, *The Evening Sentinel*, as well as a celebrated local historian with a

Another canal serving tramway, also using edged plates and flangeless wagon wheels, but of a much smaller gauge. This one took coal from Bunkers Hill Colliery at Talke Pits, north of the Potteries, to the Trent and Mersey Canal at Townfield Lock Wharf; this is where it passed under the NSR Kidsgrove to Crewe line just south of Lawton Junction. The line was a double track rope-hauled affair, with the weight of the loaded tubs going down to the canal hauling the empties back up to the colliery. Loaded tubs can be seen on the right, and empty ones under the bridge to the left (notice the primitive point work in the foreground). Bunkers Hill Colliery is presumed to date from around 1775, the date of the battle of Bunkers Hill, but it was early in the 1800s before it became very much developed, and in 1885 connection was made with the main line railway network via the NSR Audley line, thereby to some extent rendering this tubway obsolete. Nevertheless, it appears to have remained in use until about 1900 – this picture would date from the 1890s. (Map 1)

number of books on the locality to his credit. I would also like to thank the Horace Barks Reference Library at Hanley for access to the RC McGowan collection of mining photographs; McGowan was an accomplished local Mining Engineer. The Library contains much else of local industrial interest, including copies of Society Journals.

All photographs are individually acknowledged, and where none is shown then they are either from my own collection or of my own taking. Almost last, and by no means least my old friend, almost from schoolboy days, Mike Fell. Mike has once again acted as chief critic and proof reader and has, I hope readers will agree, done an excellent job. A lot of the photographs were taken on outings in the company of Mike, and many of the other older views were acquired when we were together busy 'gaffering' some old employees or whatever. I recall that at one time Mike 'courted' one of the Holditch colliery locomotive drivers daughter's, which of course, made us

welcome on and about the engines there!

But last of all, and of course it goes without saying foremost in my thoughts as I pen these few words, my wife Angela and son Kevin, who continue to put up with my absences from the norm of family life. As if my professional career as a life-long railwayman were not enough, with all the long and unsocial hours that this has over the years entailed, I then lock myself away in my study for hours on end – a very big thank you to you both!

Allan C. Baker, June 2002
Highfield House,
High Halden,
Kent.

Also by Allan Baker:
The Cheadle Railway – Oakwood Press 1979.
The Cheadle Collieries & their Railways – Trent Valley Publications 1985.
The Potteries Loop Line – Trent Valley Publications 1986.

Stoke & North Staffordshire's Railways – Irwell Press 2000.
Industrial Locomotives of North Staffordshire – Industrial Railway Society – 1997.
Birchenwood and its Locomotives – Industrial Locomotive Society – 1975.
The Industrial Locomotive – Journal of the Industrial Locomotive Society. There is a series of articles in this Journal on the locomotives, railways and other history, covering Shelton Iron & Steel Works, Holditch, Silverdale, Florence, Talk o' th' Hill and Berry Hill Collieries. They appear in the years 1976-82, and copies have been deposited in Hanley Reference Library.
Madeley & Leycett Collieries – Special Edition of the Industrial Railway Record – Journal of the Industrial Railway Society – No 161 - 2000.

Rather primitive coal winding shafts at Harriseahead Colliery, near Newchapel and north of Stoke-on-Trent. In 1921 105 men and boys were employed underground here, and 22 above. Notice the large size of the coal piled up in the foreground, and how clean it appears despite the fact that there were no washing facilities here. The two shafts are side by side, and the cage of one shaft is at the surface. Operations ceased here in the mid-1920s. (Map 2) Photograph William Jack.

Introduction

The six towns and '60 villages' that form the conurbation of the City of Stoke-on-Trent occupy approximately twenty square miles of North Staffordshire. The area is one of the most concentrated, and perhaps the most notable, products of the Industrial Revolution. In the development of its pottery and china wares, for which it is famous the world over, it is second to none. Colloquially known as 'the Potteries' for obvious reasons, it is I think the only part of the British Isles to be known by the name of its principal products. Indeed, many of the old 'finger post' road signs in the surrounding villages still direct travellers to 'The Potteries'. Grouping the Potteries with the adjacent loyal and ancient Borough of Newcastle-under-Lyme and a few other outlying areas, this book attempts to cover, largely pictorially, the heavy industry that grew out of the need for coal to fuel the pottery ovens.

Burslem is generally accepted as the 'Mother' town of the Potteries, the six towns and numerous villages that were formed into a 'Federation' in 1911. This was followed in 1926 when the status of a City was conferred upon the Federation by King George V. Until quite recent times, Stoke-on-Trent was the only city in this country that did not have a cathedral. Betraying these origins to this day, the six towns display evidence of their former independence in the form of individual Town Halls, and other provincial trappings. That famous son of the Potteries, the novelist Arnold Bennett, used the locality of his youth as the setting for many of his writings and most true 'Potters' (as we natives are known) have never forgiven him for dubbing the area 'The Five Towns'. There are of course *six*: Stoke itself (Stoke-upon-Trent, as opposed to the City of Stoke-on-Trent), Hanley, Burslem, Longton, Fenton and Tunstall – Bennett left out Fenton, the smallest. Today, despite all six towns retaining something of a town centre, Hanley has effectively developed as the 'City Centre', and for many years it has sported by far the largest shopping centre.

The first developments of a thriving pottery industry date back to the latter part of the 17th, and the early part of the 18th century, and it was the discovery of suitable deposits of clay and marl that enabled it to develop. To convert the clay into useful pottery utensils required much heat, and large quantities of coal were needed; this too, was to be found locally and in abundance. Several different types of clay and marl were discovered, and from these various differing types of pottery ware were developed. Several of these types became household names in both the industry, and with its customers. However, it was perhaps the greatest potter of them all, Josiah Wedgwood (1730-95) with whom we should start our story.

Wedgwood was one of the principal protagonists of the inland waterways of this country, suffering with his fellow 'Potters' much damage to his finished products when transported by packhorse to their markets. A native of Burslem and largely self-educated, he soon commenced business on his own and did much to develop China clay as an adjunct to the local clays and marls; this of course was not available locally and needed transporting to Staffordshire from faraway Cornwall.

The Maryhill Colliery of Harecastle Collieries Ltd at Kidsgrove developed out of a series of small footrails, and was some way up the hillside towards Rookery. Coal was brought down to the screening plant and standard gauge rail access by a narrow gauge rope-hauled tramway, using the actual pit tubs. Here is the standard gauge shunting locomotive, a 1923 Peckett 0-4-0 saddle tank (works number 1606) appropriately named MARYHILL, shunting some interesting dumb buffered hopper wagons belonging to nearby Birchenwood Colliery, about 1928. These wagons would take coal from Maryhill to Birchenwood, for subsequent coking at the latter's Coking Ovens, a transfer which involved a movement of only a few hundred yards over the main line. The engine shed is in the background. Maryhill Colliery itself closed in 1930, following a large inrush of water, and on closure of the last adjacent footrail (known elsewhere in the country as drift mines or adits and always pronounced 'footrill' in North Staffordshire) in November 1939, operations on the site ceased completely. (Map 1) Photograph the late H.W. Robinson, Industrial Railway Society Collection.

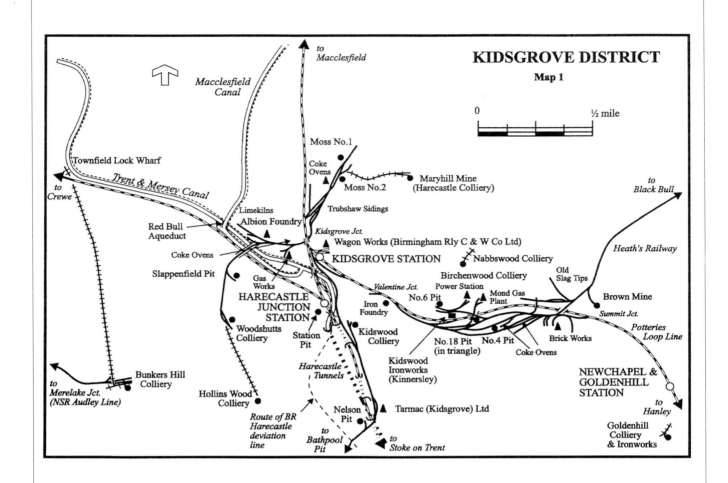

He also introduced ball clay from Dorset and flints from Newhaven. As well as this he was responsible for introducing 'true' steam power to the area. As far as is known, Wedgwood ordered the first such engine for use in North Staffordshire from Boulton & Watt, of the Soho Foundry Birmingham in 1782. This engine was built to the Boulton and Watt 'Sun & Planet Wheel' patent and though earlier engines are known to have existed in the area they worked on the 'Newcomen' atmospheric principle. The engine Wedgwood purchased was put to work in 1784 at the Etruria factory, to power a clay mill, flint mill and smaller colour-grinding pans. Others soon followed, both at Etruria and at other pottery manufactories, as well as coalmines and later iron works.

It was somewhat natural therefore, that Wedgwood got to know the local and self-made engineer James Brindley, and thus became a supporter of the embryonic Grand Trunk Canal, of which Brindley was Engineer. This was a great scheme, the country's first trunk canal and intended to connect the rivers Trent and Mersey, and provide inland transport through a most prosperous and developing part of the country. Once the route of this great undertaking was established, passing as it did right through the middle of the area, Wedgwood built a

new factory, along with a village to house his workers. Being a great enthusiast for the work of the ancient Etruscans, he chose for 'his' village and factory the name Etruria. As I am sure is well known to readers, the Grand Trunk Canal became the country's first man-made trunk waterway (hence its name) and was completed as a through route in 1777. This was in fact some years after Brindley's death, completion having been delayed by the then enormous task of tunnelling the 2,880 yards through Harecastle Hill, a ridge of high ground on which stood the northernmost of the Pottery towns and villages, and which effectively forms a barrier between North Staffordshire and the Cheshire Plain. The industrial revolution in North Staffordshire had started in earnest with the opening of this canal, which later became known more prosaically as the Trent and Mersey.

Interestingly, the Trent and Mersey was not the first canal in North Staffordshire, albeit only by a small margin, and this distinction belongs to Gresley's Canal – as it became known – dating from the year before the Trent and Mersey. This canal was built by Sir Nigel Gresley (6th Bart) and his son Nigel Bower Gresley (7th Bart), and ran some three miles from their Apedale estate, which was to the north, north-west of Newcastle-under-Lyme

to a basin alongside the Liverpool Road, which was but a half-mile from the town centre. Its purpose was to transport coal from the Gresleys' Apedale mines for sale in Newcastle, or onward transport via the Liverpool Road. Incidentally this road was Turnpiked in 1714. A further canal branching from the Trent and Mersey in Stoke opened about 1800, to serve the town of Newcastle. This was the Newcastle-under-Lyme Canal, which ran for four miles and terminated at Brook Street Wharf, to the west of the town.

About this time there also came the Newcastle-under-Lyme Junction Canal, built by the Heathcotes. R E Heathcote married Emma Sophia, second daughter of Sir Nigel Bower Gresley (who had died in 1808) and succeeded to the Apedale estate. The canal ran but one and one eighth miles from just short of the terminus of Gresley's canal, slightly north of Newcastle itself, to a terminus at Stubbs Walks south of the town. The basin here was directly parallel with the terminus of the Newcastle-under-Lyme Canal, albeit some distance away and at a higher level. There were plans for an inclined plane to connect the two but nothing ever happened in this connection, and as a result the Junction Canal never carried much other than local traffic, and in any

Between about 1922 and 1932, Tarmac (Kidsgrove) Limited, a subsidiary of Tarmac Limited, had an operation at Kidsgrove on land to the east of the NSR main line, partly over the Harecastle Tunnels. Its purpose was to recover and process, principally for road making, the old ironworks slag dumped thereabouts, from the days when there was on iron works at nearby Clough Hall. To perform the shunting here, Tarmac (Kidsgrove) Ltd hired for a period one of the Robert Heath four-wheel locomotives from the Biddulph Valley Ironworks, itself connected with the Clough Hall site by private railway. The locomotive seen here shunting the plant is Heath's No.8, actually built in 1885 by Falcon of Loughborough; it became the prototype of a further twelve similar locomotives built at Black Bull by Heath's themselves. This picture dates from around 1931. (Map 1) Photograph the late H.W. Robinson, Industrial Railway Society Collection.

event little of any sort beyond Newcastle itself.

Branches from the Trent and Mersey followed, notably to Burslem, three eighths of a mile and opened in 1805. Then came the Caldon Canal, a relatively large undertaking, especially in view of the terrain it had to traverse and its consequent engineering works. Surveyed by Brindley – who died in 1772 well before it was even started – he is said to have

One of the largest colliery and ancillary operations in North Staffordshire was that of the Birchenwood Colliery Co. Ltd at Kidsgrove, which consisted of a large colliery, several adjoining smaller pits, a coking plant, by-product recovery operations and a brick works. In the years immediately prior to the First World War this was one of the most modern coking and by-product recovery operations in the country, and visitors came from far and wide. This general view of the complex, with Kidsgrove Bank in the foreground, looks south-east. The building on the right is the German-designed Luhrig coal washer and screening plant, with the headgear of the No.18 pit shaft in the centre; this was the principal coal-winding shaft of the colliery operations. At the extreme right can just be seen the chimney for one of the main site boiler houses; the coke ovens are out of sight behind the buildings. (Map 1)

Laying the foundations of the German Luhrig mechanical coal washer and screening plant at Birchenwood about 1898. View looks due south, and to the left is part of the 1896-built battery of 124 beehive coke ovens, which had replaced several even earlier batteries. Each of these ovens could yield five tons of coke from six tons of coal, but it look four days to do it, and there was little or no recovery of any coal by-products. Modern by-product recovery ovens eventually replaced them in 1909. (Map 1)

brought about his death while engaged on the survey work, due to being outside for long periods in inclement weather; a measure of his enthusiasm. The Caldon Canal, built to serve the limestone quarries at Caldon Low on the Staffordshire/Derbyshire border, left the Summit level of the Trent and Mersey at Etruria, and ran some 17½ miles to Froghall in the Churnet Valley. Onward connection to the quarries was by a tramroad, some three miles long and authorised by the same Act as the canal. The Caldon Canal opened in 1779, with a branch to serve the Staffordshire Moorland market town of Leek (2¾ miles opened 1802) and the Norton Green Branch serving

South of the main plant at Birchenwood and to the west, alongside the NSR main line south through the Harecastle Tunnels, was the Kidswood Shaft, an upcast shaft. Its principal purpose was ventilation of the main workings, and a Waddle 25ft diameter patent fan was capable of discharging 100,000 cubic feet of air per minute. It ran at 100 rpm, and was powered by a single cylinder horizontal steam engine, with a 22in x 24in cylinder. The fan and its house are seen here under construction on 2 April 1900. Put simply, a ventilation fan drew air UP through the upcast shaft, dragging it DOWN through another shaft (the downcast shaft) and along the course of the workings in between. (Map 1)

Top of the West Slant incline rope haulage, underground at No.18 pit Birchenwood, about 1910. A row of tubs is just about to descend to the left; note haulage ropes and pulleys and how spacious it was in this part of the workings. Nonetheless, in general terms the underground workings at Birchenwood were extremely cramped, and the coal seams very shallow. This made it very difficult to mechanise coal extraction with the equipment of the day, and contributed to closure of the colliery on economic grounds. The last coal was drawn in April 1931. (Map 1) Photograph McGowan Collection, Hanley Reference Library.

Cockshead Colliery. This was about a quarter of a mile long and dated from 1805. Later, in 1866 or thereabouts, came the Foxley Branch, often confused with the Norton Green Branch, built to serve Norton Colliery and ironworks at Ford Green. Five eighths of a mile long, the ironworks here belonged to Robert Heath and dated from the same time as the Foxley Branch.

In 1811 the Caldon Canal was extended 13¼ miles southwards along the Churnet Valley as the Uttoxeter Canal, to serve that town. Then there was the one and half mile Hall Green

This is the West Slant electric endless haulage engine and drums, at the No.18 pit Birchenwood, about 1910. The motor is a 250hp Mather & Platt AC machine, driving twin 7ft diameter cast iron surge drums, and an 8ft diameter rope drum. After closure, at the sale of the colliery equipment here in October 1931, this equipment fetched the princely sum of £37 10s; unfortunately we know not who bought it, but it may have just gone for scrap. (Map 1) Photograph McGowan Collection, Hanley Reference Library.

Part of the Birchenwood steam power station (there was a gas engine powered one too) about 1910. There are three identical generating sets to be seen here, each consisting of a Bellis & Morcom vertical two cylinder compound steam engine and Mather & Platt alternator. The engines each had 19in and 27in diameter by 12in stroke cylinders, fed with steam at 90 psi; the alternators ran at 375 rpm, and delivered 350 kW at 2,600 volts, being three phase 50 cycle machines. As well as these engines and the gas engine driven generating plant, there were two Bellis-Siemens turbo-alternator sets, each rated at 1,000 kW, with compound mixed pressure impulse turbines driving the alternators, which in turn delivered three phase 50 cycles current at 2,600 volts, running at 1,470 rpm. (Map 1) Photograph McGowan Collection, Hanley Reference Library.

Branch from the Trent and Mersey main course at Kidsgrove. This was built to make an end on connection with the Macclesfield Canal and opened at the same time, in 1831. This short branch also served to protect the Trent and Mersey Canal's water, by ensuring that none could flow from it to the Macclesfield Canal, but rather the other way round. Canal companies were famously protective of their water supplies, and for good reason it has to

The year 1909 saw the commissioning at Birchenwood of a battery of 84 Simon-Carves by-product recovery coke ovens, to replace the earlier beehive installation. Consisting of sixty ovens of the waste heat type, and twenty-four with complete by-product recovery, an extensive by-product recovery plant was built at the same time. In 1912, a further battery of ovens was built, this time consisting of seventy-two Carl Still ovens of German manufacture, in twin sets of thirty-six each, with full by-product recovery. The combined output following commissioning of this battery amounted to 4,500 tons of coke per week, making Birchenwood one of the largest coking plants in the country. Most of the coke went to the Biddulph Valley ironworks of the parent Company, Robert Heath & Sons Limited. This photograph shows the coke 'pusher' of the Simon Calves battery; its function was to push the coke out of the ovens when it was ready. It was on rails and electrically powered, so as to be able to move alongside whichever oven needed pushing. Likewise, the coke wagon running on rails on the opposite side of the ovens would be manoeuvred so as to catch the coke as it emerged. (Map 1) Photograph McGowan Collection, Hanley Reference Library.

General view of the No.18 pit at Birchenwood and associated buildings shortly after closure of the colliery in 1931. Left to right are the pit headgear and screens, pumping engine house, and Luhrig coal washer. The left-hand chimney served the Carl Still ovens, the middle one the Simon Carves ovens, and the right-hand one the colliery boiler house. To the left of the boiler house chimney is the headgear of the No.4 pit, a downcast shaft used for drainage and ventilation purposes. The main drainage pump was at No.18 (also a downcast pit); it had a 'Cornish' condensing beam engine with a 72in diameter cylinder and an 8ft 6in stroke. With 32ft cast iron beam, it fittingly rejoiced in the name GOLIATH. (Map 1) Photograph William Jack.

be added. The Macclesfield Canal ran 26½ miles from Hall Green, through Macclesfield to Marple. Some of these canals were subsequently used as the formations for railways, notably the Uttoxeter Canal; acquired by the embryo North Staffordshire Railway (NSR) in 1847, part of it was used for the route of the NSR Churnet Valley Railway. Parts of the Newcastle-under-Lyme Junction Canal too, were used, as the formation for the NSR line when it was extended westwards from Newcastle to Apedale in 1851. Of the remainder of these waterways the Newcastle-under-Lyme Canal closed in part in 1921 and completely in 1935 – it had been leased to the NSR from 1863. The Burslem Branch fell out of use quite late, and was still navigable in the 1950s, while the Foxley arm

Final stages in the erection of a new battery of seventeen Simon Calves coke ovens, replacing the earlier ones of this make that had ceased production in 1926. This picture, taken on 10 August 1938, looks south east, and in the foreground can be seen the coke discharge arrangements of the surviving Carl Still ovens, which also passed out of use once the new ones were up and running. A further fourteen ovens were added after the war in 1947, and the total of 31 ovens were then able to make 4,800 tons of coke per week, in contrast to 4,500 tons from the 146 older ovens. (Map 1)

A coke oven at Birchenwood being 'pushed', with the red-hot coke forced into the special rail vehicle. This would then be moved on and 'quenched' by the discharge of large quantities of water which stopped the combustion process. With the change over to natural gas, the operations at Birchenwood gradually became un-economic, as the bulk of the gas produced in the coking process had latterly been sold to the local Gas Board. The plant eventually closed in early 1973. (Map 1)

ceased to be used about 1934. The remainder, the Trent and Mersey, the Caldon and the Hall Green branch (and of course, the Macclesfield) remain in use today. It is interesting to recall here that the fledgling NSR acquired, under its original Acts of Incorporation, ownership of the Trent and Mersey and Caldon Canals, so stifling the vigorous competition that so bedevilled many of the other early railway companies. However, unlike many of the other railway companies, once it acquired the canals the NSR did not neglect them, but developed them as an

One of the Birchenwood fleet of locomotives, with the No.18 pit headgear to the extreme right. This is No.1 (works number 1361) an Avonside of 1896 rebuilt at the colliery in June 1912. It lasted until 1933-34, when it was scrapped. Typical of its maker's products, notice the tall elegant chimney, dome and Salter balance safety valves. To the left can be seen parts of the Mond gas producer plant, and the Loop Line cutting is behind the row of barrels. (Map 1) Photograph the late H.W. Robinson, Industrial Railway Society Collection.

Goldendale again, looking north towards Harecastle; in the centre of this view, between blast furnaces and chimney, can be seen the Blowing Engine House. This housed reciprocating beam blowing engines for the blast air to the furnaces. In later years they operated as a pair; notice the two flywheels, the one on the right-hand engine being bigger than the other. The left-hand engine dated from around 1833, coming here second-hand in 1844 and was then non-rotative. The right-hand engine, also originally non-rotative, was added later. Many parts of these engines were made at Goldendale, as the company's name was cast on several of them, and the later engine may have been built on the site in its entirety. In the 1860s they were both made rotative, and coupled so as to work permanently as a pair but in the 1930s this arrangement was altered so that they could again work separately, hence the small flywheel on the left-hand engine. The twin beams can be seen sticking out of the house, and my father used to recall how he had observed them bobbing up and down as he passed when on Police Ambulance driving and Motor Patrol duty during the War. (Map 3)

Goldendale in August 1972, a year after closure but before dismantling. View looks south and the modernised blast furnaces can be seen to dominate the centre of the illustration. To the left are the hot blast stoves, although some of the works production was made under the cold blast method until the end. This gave a particular grade of cast iron from the type of iron ore used, then in demand by internal combustion engine manufacturers. (Map 3) Photograph Allan C. Baker.

Newfields Wharf, between Tunstall and Kidsgrove and the termination of the short, 61 chain steeply graded NSR Newfields branch. Originally projected as part of a through route from Longport via Tunstall – the Tunstall Upper Branch – it was reduced to this short stub by the coming of the Potteries Loop Line, which bisected its route between Tunstall and Pitts Hill at what became Newfields Junction. Because of this, the branch connection with the Loop was via a very awkward zigzag arrangement. As can be seen from the traffic on hand here in this 29 June 1953 view, it largely served the needs of the local pottery industry and, in view of its light construction, severe axle load restrictions were applied. Hence the use of the ex-LNWR 'Cauliflower' 0-6-0 tender engine No.58382, and Stoke shed had to keep a couple of these on its allocation solely for the purpose of working this branch line. They did find other uses meantime, and many is the Stoke engineman who cut his teeth on them! The Newfields branch opened 1 October 1874 and closed 3 August 1959. (Map 3) Photograph F.W. Shuttleworth.

Parkhouse Colliery at Chesterton was served by the NSR Chesterton branch; itself a branch from the Talke branch, it ran one mile and four furlongs from Talke Junction near Chatterley to Chesterton and opened in January 1866. Parkhouse Colliery dates from the 1850s; originally sunk for ironstone, it was reached by a back shunt from the Chesterton branch – the colliery was acquired by Robert Heath & Sons Limited in July 1913. In this photograph of 29 August 1967 No.3, a Bagnall 0-6-0ST (works number 2992) of 1950, shunts while BR brings in the empties with diesel shunter No.D4109 from Stoke shed. The wagons in the centre are on the Lansdale wharf, and parts of another out of use Bagnall locomotive can just be seen to the extreme left (BERRY HILL NO.4, Bagnall No.3075 of 1954). The Chesterton branch was closed beyond the junction with the colliery on 4 June 1962, and the remainder on closure of the colliery in June 1968. (Map 4) Photograph M.G. Fell.

Aerial view at a late stage of construction of the Harecastle Tunnel diversion scheme, which opened to all traffic on 27 June 1966. This was part of the BR London Midland Region London-Manchester, Liverpool and Birmingham electrification scheme, and was necessary due to the reduced clearances in the Harecastle Tunnels. Notice at bottom left the realigned Chesterton branch, with its former course just above, and bisected by the new line, hence the need for this new connection with the main line; it opened on 18 October 1964. In between the two routes can be seen the remains of the blowing engine house of the Chatterley Ironworks, which closed in 1901 and the branch canal basin and course of the branch canal built to serve its needs. Chatterley Sidings can be seen in the right middle, and to their left the NCB Chatterley Coal Stocking Ground and sidings. The old line to Chesterton seen here after track lifting was in fact the Talke branch, built privately by local industrialist Ralph Sneyd, to serve collieries and ironworks at Talk o' th' Hill, and opened in 1860; it was leased to the NSR from July 1864. The Chesterton branch left it at Talke Junction, but in 1877 this junction was removed due to the intensity of traffic, and a second line of rails laid, such that the Talke and Chesterton branches became completely independent from the main line junction at Chatterley, but running parallel with each other to the site of the former junction. The line curving away to the extreme right in the middle serves Goldendale Ironworks, and the bridge buttresses surviving alongside the old Talke formation originally carried a line from the Ironworks to serve outlying ironstone and coal pits. The remains of the workings of this can be seen in the middle centre distance. (Map 3) Photograph Collection M.G. Fell.

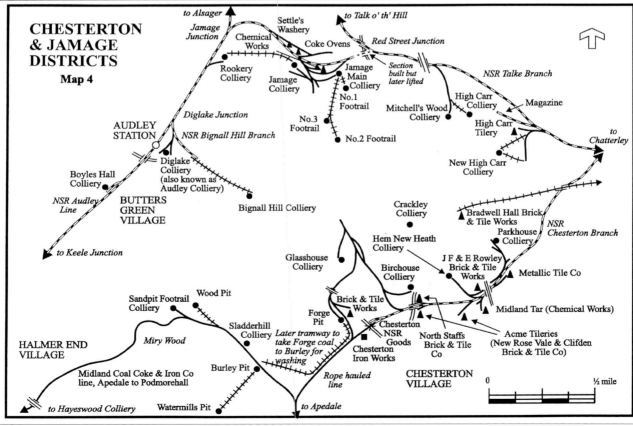

CHESTERTON & JAMAGE DISTRICTS
Map 4

to Alsager
Jamage Junction
Settle's Washery
to Talk o' th' Hill
Chemical Works
Coke Ovens
Red Street Junction
Rookery Colliery
Jamage Colliery
Jamage Main Colliery
Section built but later lifted
NSR Talke Branch
No.1 Footrail
Mitchell's Wood Colliery
High Carr Colliery
Magazine
Diglake Junction
No.3 Footrail
No.2 Footrail
High Carr Tilery
AUDLEY STATION
NSR Bignall Hill Branch
New High Carr Colliery
to Chatterley
Boyles Hall Colliery
Diglake Colliery (also known as Audley Colliery)
Bignall Hill Colliery
Crackley Colliery
Bradwell Hall Brick & Tile Works
NSR Chesterton Branch
Parkhouse Colliery
NSR Audley Line
BUTTERS GREEN VILLAGE
Hem New Heath Colliery
J F & E Rowley Brick & Tile Works
Metallic Tile Co
to Keele Junction
Glasshouse Colliery
Birchouse Colliery
Midland Tar (Chemical Works)
Sandpit Footrail Colliery
Wood Pit
Brick & Tile Works
Forge Pit
Chesterton NSR Goods
North Staffs Brick & Tile Co
Acme Tileries (New Rose Vale & Clifden Brick & Tile Co)
HALMER END VILLAGE
Sladderhill Colliery
Miry Wood
Later tramway to take Forge coal to Burley for washing
Chesterton Iron Works
CHESTERTON VILLAGE
Midland Coal Coke & Iron Co line, Apedale to Podmorehall
Burley Pit
Rope hauled line
0   ½ mile
to Hayeswood Colliery
Watermills Pit
to Apedale

General view of Talk o' th' Hill Colliery in the early 1900s, looking due north with the small settlement of Foxholes behind, to the right of the right-hand chimney. The villages of Talke Pits and Talke itself are off the picture to the right, all some four miles north of Newcastle-under-Lyme. The then owner, Ralph Sneyd, connected this pit and an ironworks (closed in 1873) to the main line railway system by a private railway built in 1860. It was leased to the NSR by an Act of 1864, and sold to them in 1904. In its early years the Colliery Company also worked its own workmen's trains to convey its men at shift changes to and from Chatterley. The colliery here was the scene of one of the area's worst ever mining disasters, when no less than 91 men and boys lost their lives in a firedamp explosion, on 13 December 1866. In this photograph taken from the top of the battery of seventy Simon Carves by-product coke ovens, to the right can be seen one of the two sets of headgear, and to the right of that the wagon and locomotive repair shops. The colliery here closed in March 1928, and over 1,000 men and boys were put out of work. (Maps 3-4)

Underground at Talk o' th' Hill showing one of the principal roadways. Notice the endless rope haulage system, with the ropes lying in the narrow gauge tracks, wooden timber support system and the metal netting lining each side. Behind this netting were large quantities of stone dust known as a stone dust barrier, the purpose being to reduce the extent of any firedamp (gas) explosions. In the event of an explosion, the dust would become dispersed, and have the effect of reducing any resulting fireball, and hopefully also reduce potential casualties and damage. This roadway was to gain access to the Longwall level as it was known, and the Two Row coal – 'Longwall' took its name from the system of working the coal. The method of working with an endless rope was to attach the wagons or tubs to the continuously running rope by quick release devices, the rope itself running along both inward and outward railways, with a return pulley at its far end. (Maps 3-4) Photograph McGowan Collection, Hanley Reference Library.

One of the oldest ironworks in North Staffordshire was that at Silverdale, north-west of Newcastle, with blast furnaces in operation by 1786. There had however, been iron making on this site for many years before that, and there were associated collieries, forges and foundries. The land hereabouts was a part of the Sneyd estate, and Ralph Sneyd (1793-1870) is prominent in the industrial history of North Staffordshire during the Industrial Revolution and its aftermath. Indeed his lessees promoted some of the earliest private railways in the area, on land he owned. In 1849-50, Francis Stanier, being a Sneyd business partner in the Silverdale operation, built a railway two miles and 28 chains long, The Silverdale & Newcastle-under-Lyme Railway, from Silverdale to the Pool Dam at Newcastle. At the time this line was unconnected with any other railway, and served to take Silverdale coal and iron to Newcastle for sale as well as onward transport by the Newcastle Canal. The line did not extend to the canal itself, terminating some half a mile short of the basin, doubtless as this further

distance was not on Sneyd land. Goods had to be transhipped by horse and cart this half mile, but it did not take the Canal Company long to promote the grandiosely titled Newcastle-under-Lyme Canal Extension Railway, whose meagre half-mile of track came into use some time in 1854. This photograph, dating from around 1880, shows the furthest point of Stanier's Railway, at what was known as the Furnace Bank.

Note to the left two open topped blast furnaces employing cold blast, with charging hoist, boilers in front and blowing engine house and chimney alongside. To the right of the engine house can be seen a row of workmen's cottages, with the Foreman's house in front, and further to the right the chimney of the adjacent forges and foundries. (Map 5) Photograph Collection the late Dr J.R. Hollick.

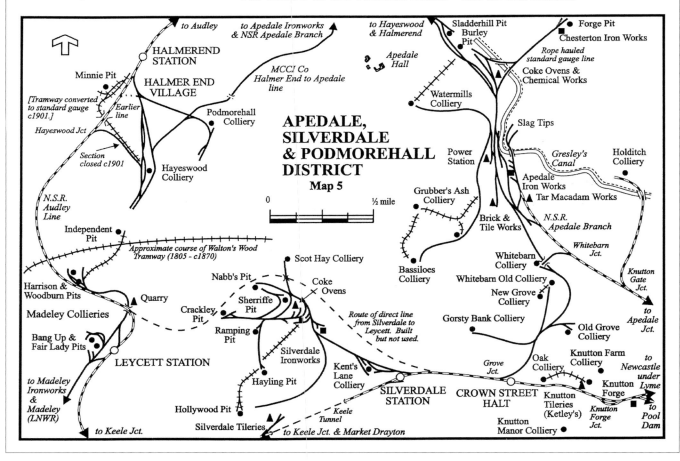

Kents Lane No.17 pit at Silverdale about 1905; this shaft was 8ft in diameter and sunk to the depth of 135 yards, principally to reach and extract the Blackband ironstone. This was a famous and much sought after ironstone with, for the locality, a comparatively high yield. In the middle distance it is being 'calcined' and then loaded via the chutes into standard gauge wagons. 'Calcining' is a process of concentrating iron ore by burning off the moisture, carbon dioxide and so on, thus oxidizing the ore ready for smelting in the blast furnace. In 1918, the colliery operations here passed to the ownership of the Shelton Iron Steel & Coal Company Limited. View looks north-east; observe the nice collection of private owner wagons, and the spare engine flywheel on the bank. (Map 5) Photograph Collection the late Dr J.R. Hollick.

A later view of the No.17 pit at Kents Lane, with a new all-steel headgear in place. Notice how the size of the dirt tip behind the headsticks has grown in the intervening period, and that some demolition work in underway in the foreground. The exhaust from the engine house indicates that the engine was in the act of winding the cages when the photograph was taken. (Map 5)

In 1890 a fusion of two companies took place when the ironworks, collieries and ancillary operations at Apedale and the collieries at Halmerend (the latter in the ownership of Cooper & Craig) were combined to form the Midland Coal Coke & Iron Company Limited. To assist operations and to save NSR transport charges the new company built a private line, The Apedale & Podmore Hall Railway, to connect the two sites – it was a little over two miles long and opened in the late 1890s. Coal from the Podmore Hall collieries at Halmerend could then be taken to Apedale for coking, or onwards if it was heading east, rather then incur NSR charges for the circuitous route via Keele and Silverdale. This picture shows the Podmore Hall No.3 pits, looking west towards the open country and Shropshire. There are two sets of headgear but one winding engine house; note the large fan duct to the extreme left – its fan was 25ft diameter, and made by Walker Brothers of Wigan. Wagons are being loaded in the foreground – there were no screening or washing facilities here, such operations being undertaken at Apedale. Like many industrial concerns, not least in North Staffordshire, the combine came on hard times between the wars and the entire operations at both Apedale and Podmore Hall closed in April 1930, throwing thousands of men out of work. (Map 5)

Right. The Minnie Pit at Halmerend, seen here on its opening day in 1881, was named after its owner, W.Y. Craig's daughter. This was the downcast shaft for the Podmore Hall operations, 359 yards deep to the 4ft, 5ft, 7ft, Banbury and Bullhurst coals and in its day an extremely profitable pit for its owners. It was the scene of North Staffordshire's worst ever mining disaster when, on 12 January 1918, a terrific explosion rent the Bullhurst and Banbury workings, taking with it the lives of no less than 155 men and boys, some as young as 14 years. If that were not enough, Hugh Doorbar, Captain of the Birchenwood No.1 Rescue Team, lost his life during the rescue operations on 14 January, and it was not until the middle of the following year before all the bodies were recovered. The cause was attributed to the phenomenon of 'after damp', an explosive mixture which follows earlier explosions but the source of the ignition was never firmly established. The Minnie Pit never again reached it previous outputs, and it closed along with the rest of the combine in 1930. Today, a monument stands on the capped shaft, in memory of all those who lost their lives on that terrible day, so many years ago and at a time when so many of their contemporaries were giving their lives for their country in distant parts. (Map 5)

The Minnie Pit was separated from the main Podmore Hall complex by the NSR Audley line. This had opened from Keele (where it left the Silverdale to Market Drayton line) to Alsager, joining the line from Kidsgrove to Crewe, on 24 July 1870 (28 June 1880 for passengers). The line connecting the pits went under the NSR formation just south of Halmerend Station, at two miles 44 chains from Keele. This view shows the connecting line looking towards the Minnie Pit; a single line standard gauge railway, it used rope haulage at this period – the view dates from about 1890. (Map 5)

Aerial view of the Knutton Forge of the Knutton Iron & Steel Company Limited, situated between Newcastle-under-Lyme and Silverdale. This lay west of the NSR line between these two places, which can be seen running horizontally across the picture. The line curving around behind the works is the Pool Dam branch, part of the original Silverdale & Newcastle-under-Lyme Railway, as built by Stanier. The village of Knutton can be seen to top right, and the road in the foreground is the main thoroughfare from Newcastle to Silverdale. The forge dates from about 1855, and closed the year after the Apedale Complex, of which it was a subsidiary. The Apedale locomotives had running powers over the NSR and later the LMS, between Apedale and the Forge, as well as to Pool Dam – a lot of the iron produced at Apedale was processed here. The Silverdale locomotives also had running powers between Silverdale and Pool Dam. (Map 5)

Pair of Walkers of Wigan, cross compound steam air compressors at the Whitfield Colliery powerhouse, on 21 November 1970. These engines, located adjacent to the Hesketh Pit of 1915, exhausted into the mixed pressure turbine alternator set, to be seen above them and slightly to the right. When this photograph was taken they were all out of use, and awaiting scrapping. (Map2) Photograph Allan C. Baker.

Pinnox Junction about 1905, where the Whitfield Pinnox Mineral Railway joined the NSR Pinnox branch (often referred to in 'official' NSR literature as The Spur Line) seen here to the right – roughly midway between Longport and Tunstall. The over bridge in the background took the mineral railway from Pinnox Sidings to Greenhead Wharf at Burslem, a very steeply graded line where engines propelled but two or three wagons at a time. The NSR 'D' class 0-6-0 tank No.139 – built by the Company at Stoke in 1893 – is about to leave with a loaded train for Longport Junction, where a larger engine would doubtless take over for the journey via Crewe, and possibly onwards to Liverpool, Garston or Birkenhead docks for export. A lot of Chatterley Whitfield coal was destined for export via one of these ports. (Map 3)

Top left. Robert Heath had a second large series of operations in the Biddulph Valley at Ford Green; this is the ironworks through the bridge taking the Hanley to Leek road (present A53) over the NSR line at Foxley. There was also a branch from the Caldon Canal to serve the works; this was the Foxley branch, and some remains can still be seen to this day despite it having fallen out of use very many years ago. The Caldon Canal, by the way, was itself a branch from the Trent and Mersey, which it left at the Summit Lock at Etruria. View looks north and the signal is the Milton Junction down starter, Milton Junction being behind the photographer, and where the line to Leek left the Biddulph Valley line. Notice the four open topped blast furnaces, chimneys and hot blast stoves, so nicely framed by the bridge – also the NSR level crossing keeper's house, there being a level crossing here before the bridge was built. Operations commenced at Ford Green in 1854, and Heath's took over in 1860; the photograph dates from the 1890s. (Map 6)

Bottom left. Looking north along the Biddulph Valley line, at Ford Green. The bridge carries a private Robert Heath mineral railway from the ironworks and collieries to further pits at Holden Lane and a land sale wharf at the top of Smallthorne Bank, at Nettlebank. This line took a zigzag route to ease the steep gradient but even so it was 1 in 16 in places, and the Robert Heath-built four wheeled locomotives managed to propel but two loaded wagons at a time up the line. Notice iron ore for the ironworks in the wagons to the left, Ford Green station along with the signal box and footbridge in the distance, and the NSR 'D' class 0-6-0 side tank engaged in shunting the spur into the works. The Biddulph Valley line opened between Stoke and Congleton on 28 August 1860, with passenger traffic introduced on 1 June 1864. It closed to passenger traffic 11 July 1927. (Map 6)

Right. Norton Colliery at Ford Green in the 1930s, with its tandem head gear for the upcast shafts to the left, and the all steel head gear for the downcast and main coal winding shaft to the right. Notice the carefully arranged stack of coal and Norton in the Moors village on the skyline. The ironworks and later steel making plant here closed in 1928, along with the operations at Black Bull but Norton Colliery, along with the pits at Black Bull, were formed into a new company, Norton & Biddulph Collieries Limited. This firm passed into NCB ownership at nationalisation of the coal industry on 1 January 1947. (Map 6) Photograph William Jack.

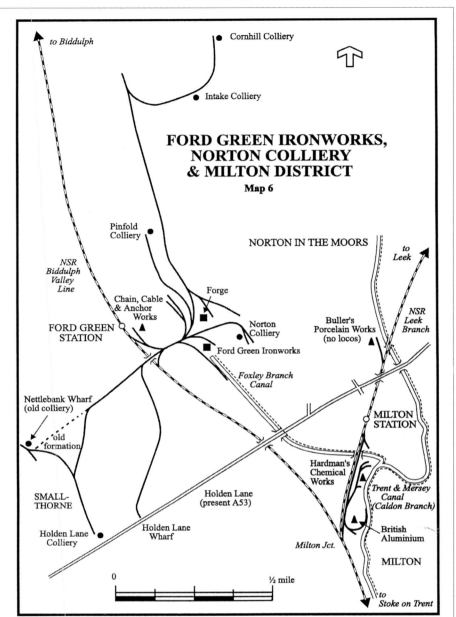

FORD GREEN IRONWORKS, NORTON COLLIERY & MILTON DISTRICT

Map 6

One of the 'home made' Robert Heath (Black Bull) four wheelers at Norton about 1935. This one is No.9, one of the last built and dating from 1926. Judging by the amount of coal stacked on the footplate the engine would be engaged on the Nettlebank job, but she later migrated to Victoria Colliery at Black Bull, and was scrapped there in September 1964. The line to Nettlebank was closed on 1 May 1953. (Map 6) Photograph J.H.L. Adams Collection, Late R.G. Jarvis, Midland Railway Trust.

Norton Colliery on 12 April 1977, with Ruston & Hornsby six wheel diesel hydraulic locomotive VICTORIA D1 (maker's number 512844 of 1965) shunting. Formerly at Victoria Colliery Black Bull, it came here in March 1976, almost at the end, for the pit closed on 23 June 1977, the workings having been connected underground with Wolstanton Colliery. In 1947 407,000 tons of coal were drawn here, with 1,346 men employed. (Map 6) Photograph Allan C. Baker.

One of the most progressive pits in North Staffordshire between the wars was Sneyd Colliery at Burslem, seen here in the 1930s. Dating from about 1849, coal mining in this area goes back much earlier, and by 1924 there were four shafts in use. In 1927 1,650 men and boys were employed underground, with a further 540 above, and between 1931 and 1945 annual output averaged 488,000 tons. This view looks south-east, with the No.4 shaft to the right; this was the principal coal winder, 15ft in diameter to a depth of 890 yards. To the left is the No.2 shaft, an upcast of 13ft 6in diameter and 621 yards deep. On New Years Day 1942, this colliery was the scene of an underground explosion, when a train of run away tubs caused sparking which in turn ignited coal dust; 57 men lost their lives. Mercifully this was the last mining disaster in North Staffordshire to claim a double figure death toll. (Map 7) Photograph William Jack.

Sneyd was famous among industrial railway enthusiasts in employing one of only four 'industrial' Garratt articulated locomotives to have operated in this country. SNEYD COLLIERIES Ld No 3 was built by Beyer Peacock in 1931 – maker's number 6729 – and was purchased in view of the extremely difficult rail layout in the pit yard. Situated on rising ground between Burslem and Smallthorne, it abounded in steep gradients and sharp curves, making an articulated locomotive ideal for the job. Here she is when almost new, and some idea of the difficulties can be gained from this photograph. (Map 7)

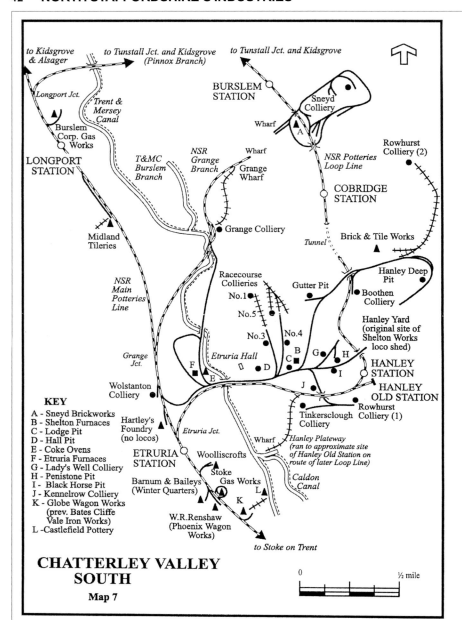

to Kidsgrove & Alsager

to Tunstall Jct. and Kidsgrove (Pinnox Branch)

to Tunstall Jct. and Kidsgrove

Longport Jct.

Trent & Mersey Canal

BURSLEM STATION

Sneyd Colliery

Wharf

A

Burslem Corp. Gas Works

LONGPORT STATION

T&MC Burslem Branch

NSR Grange Branch

Wharf

Grange Wharf

NSR Potteries Loop Line

Rowhurst Colliery (2)

COBRIDGE STATION

Midland Tileries

Grange Colliery

Tunnel

Brick & Tile Works

NSR Main Potteries Line

Racecourse Collieries
No.1

Gutter Pit

Hanley Deep Pit

Boothen Colliery

No.5

Hanley Yard (original site of Shelton Works loco shed)

No.3

No.4

Grange Jct.

Etruria Hall

B
C

G

H

F

D

E

I

HANLEY STATION

Wolstanton Colliery

J

HANLEY OLD STATION

KEY
A - Sneyd Brickworks
B - Shelton Furnaces
C - Lodge Pit
D - Hall Pit
E - Coke Ovens
F - Etruria Furnaces
G - Lady's Well Colliery
H - Penistone Pit
I - Black Horse Pit
J - Kennelrow Colliery
K - Globe Wagon Works
   (prev. Bates Cliffe
   Vale Iron Works)
L - Castlefield Pottery

Hartley's Foundry (no locos)

Etruria Jct.

Tinkersclough Colliery

Rowhurst Colliery (1)

Wharf

Hanley Plateway (ran to approximate site of Hanley Old Station on route of later Loop Line)

ETRURIA STATION

Woolliscrofts

Stoke Gas Works

Caldon Canal

Barnum & Baileys (Winter Quarters)

L

K

W.R.Renshaw (Phoenix Wagon Works)

to Stoke on Trent

CHATTERLEY VALLEY SOUTH

Map 7

0   ½ mile

Top right. Wolstanton Colliery in 1948, a view looking east with the ore preparation plant of the Shelton Iron & Steel Works behind. This pit was owned and developed in pre-nationalisation days by the Lilleshall Company Limited of Okengates in Shropshire; latterly owned by a consortium of local pottery owners, it dated from the period 1916-19. It was much developed by the NCB from about 1960, and eventually took over the underground workings of Sneyd, Hanley Deep Pit, Chatterley Whitfield and Norton Collieries, all the output being drawn here. However, despite high hopes, in only one year did output reach the magical one million tons, which was its *raison d'être.* Thereafter there was a steady decline and by 1970 only 625,000 tons were produced, with a labour force of 1,349 men. There was a further decline to 458,000 tons with 1,219 men in the period 1981-82. Closure came in October 1985, hastened by the prolonged Miners Strike. On the skyline from left to right are the dirt tips of no less than five other collieries. They are, Chatterley Whitfield (this pit was in a valley, but remember it was perhaps the largest dirt tip in the country!); Sneyd (two tips); Norton in the distance between the two belonging to Sneyd; Hanley Deep Pit and Racecourse – this latter pit had closed in 1941. The twin headgears between the last two tips mark the site of Hanley Deep Pit Colliery. (Map 7) Photograph E.J.D. Warrillow, Keele University Library Collection.

Left. The Garratt at the end of its life, on 4 April 1962, with Moorland Road (the main road between Burslem and Smallthorne) in the background. Although generally successful, the engine proved expensive to maintain and despite being able to do the work of two 'normal' locomotives, after nationalisation the NCB purchased conventional locomotives for use at Sneyd – indeed the colliery company itself had purchased one during the war. Hence, the Garratt was little used latterly, so Roger Hateley was lucky to see her working on this occasion. Coal winding ceased at Sneyd on 7 July 1962. Unfortunately, nobody wanted the Garratt and she was cut up for scrap at Sneyd in January 1963. (Map 7) Photograph Roger Hateley.

The largest gas works in North Staffordshire, and one that eventually superseded all the other local ones, was at Etruria, with a history going back to 1825. Between 1898 and 1904 this works was extensively developed and largely moved west, so as to be alongside the NSR main line between Cliffe Vale and Etruria. The first siding agreement with the NSR was dated 1904. In 1922 it became the property of Stoke-on-Trent Corporation and on nationalisation of the industry, in May 1949, part of the West Midlands Gas Board. There were further extensions, including large waterless gas holders and in 1945 it was capable of producing nine million cubic feet of gas per day – this was of course, almost the pinnacle of coal gas production for industrial and domestic purposes in this country. This view taken in 1973 shows one of the waterless gasholders, among the biggest in the county, and capable of holding five million cubic feet of gas. Like all coal gas works, Etruria succumbed to natural gas and coal gas production ceased on 20 March 1971. Almost the entire site has since been cleared with the exception of one small gas holder, and the area is now occupied by a series of small industrial units. (Map 7)

A 1949 view from the top of the gas holder in the previous view, looking north-west. At the top are the contiguous villages of Basford to the left, and May Bank to the right. In the foreground can be seen Etruscan Street, with its rows of terraced houses built for the employees of the gas works and nearby Woolliscroft's tile manufactory. To the left is Etruria Station, with its distinctive and, for the NSR, unique island platform. The main line heads away north towards the Chatterley Valley, Harecastle Hill and Kidsgrove. Etruria and Grange Junction sidings can be discerned to the upper right. Extreme left above the station can be seen Downing's 'marl hole' (local term for a clay pit) and ACME tile works, with Hartleys' foundry below. Running through the centre is the main Newcastle to Hanley Road (called Etruria Road) with Hanley to the right and the NSR Potteries Loop Line curving away from Etruria Junction to the upper right. Note especially, at the top centre, rows of prefabricated ('Prefab') single story bungalows, built as a quick cure for the post-war housing shortage. This had been made worse, of course, by bomb damage though few in fact had been dropped on the Potteries, despite the presence of the Shelton Iron & Steel Works, and much other industry besides. (Map 7) Photograph E.J.D. Warrillow, Keele University Library.

Etruria Junction in the 1930s, with an ex-LNWR 'Prince of Wales' 4-6-0, about to join the main line on a through Manchester to Birmingham train. From left to right across the middle of this photograph are the slag tips of Shelton Iron & Steel Works, the blast furnace charging hoists and gantries, the steel melting shop (the four parallel and symmetrical chimneys) and the rolling mills. Note the WEDGWOOD sign; the celebrated potter Josiah Wedgwood built his manufactory at Etruria, alongside the Trent and Mersey Canal, of which he was a principal protagonist, and the village grew up around it. Indeed, in his ambition to emulate the famous Etruscan pottery wares he gave the village he built for his workers the name Etruria. The trail of exhaust to the right of the sign doubtless marks the path of one of the steel works shunting locomotives. The gradient of the Loop Line as it left the main line here was around 1 in 50, gaining height to cross the Trent and Mersey Canal at its summit level. (Map 7) Photograph E.J.D. Warrillow Collection, Keele University Library.

Probably the largest industrial undertaking in North Staffordshire was that of the Shelton Iron Steel & Coal Company Limited at Etruria and Shelton, dating from about 1839. The first four blast furnaces are seen here about 1870; they were adjacent to the present Cobridge Road and were first 'blown' on 4 January 1841. Each was 60ft high and the hearths were 7ft diameter, the beam-blowing engine having a horsepower of 130. In 1848 these furnaces produced 7,280 tons of pig iron. The view looks west-north-west and reveals, from left to right, the iron foundry and the battery of seven Lancashire boilers immediately in front of the furnace chimney, with the furnaces themselves behind. To the right of the furnaces is the blowing engine house, and battery of beehive coke ovens, with the colliery headgear to the extreme right marking the site of the Racecourse Colliery. This colliery was so named from its its site, a former racecourse, on land acquired by Earl Granville when he commenced operations hereabouts. The brick walls in the foreground contain the cooling water for the forges and furnaces – note the rows of dumb buffered wagons, many loaded with iron ore, and the ore calcining area alongside. These furnaces were blown out for the last time in the early 1880s, replaced by developments at Etruria. (Map 7) Photograph E.J.D. Warrillow Collection, Keele University Library.

In 1853 a second set of four blast furnaces was erected at Etruria itself, on the site later occupied by the furnaces that remained in use until iron production ceased at Shelton in June 1978. View looks north-west, with the trees of Etruria Vale to be seen in the background. Notice the furnace charging hoist and platform connecting the furnace tops, hearths below and the pig beds in the foreground. The blowing engine here was of Lilleshall manufacture, as were most of the engines and boilers on site, as the Earl was also connected

with the Lilleshall Company at Oakengates in Shropshire. Main line rail connection came early to these works, the first industrial undertaking to be directly connected to the NSR, with the opening of 'Earl Granville's branch Railway' from the main line at Etruria on 10 June 1850. This later became part of the NSR Hanley branch (opened 20 December 1861) and later still part of the famous Potteries Loop Line. (Map 7) Photograph E.J.D. Warrillow Collection, Keele University Library.

Top left. The Shelton forges and mills adjacent to Mill Street (hence its name – later Etruria Road) between Etruria and Hanley. The bell topped furnaces to be seen in a semi-circle across the middle of the photograph are the wrought iron puddling furnaces. By 1872 there were 66 at this site and a further 34 at Etruria. There were also seven rolling mills, two of which can be seen to the rear of the furnaces. The pipes connecting the tops of the furnace bells are gas mains, bringing gas to fire the furnaces from the coke ovens. Notice the limestone in the wagons as well as stock piled, the heaps of pig iron to the left and, peeping out from the right of the weigh bridge house, one of the elegant Beyer Peacock saddle tank shunting engines, of which the Company had three. They dated from 1856, 1863 and 1873, the second two being named ETRURIA and LORD LEVESON (hereditary title of the son of Earl Granville) respectively. (Map 7) Photograph E.J.D. Warrillow Collection, Keele University Library.

Below. As would be expected there were several pits around the Shelton and Etruria sites, drawing both coal and ironstone. This is the Rowhurst No.2 pit in 1891. A downcast shaft of 12ft diameter and 518 yards deep, it was situated on what later became a southwards extension of Hanley railway station goods yard and is today occupied by industrial premises. In 1898 the No.1 and 2 pits (No.1 was the upcast, also 518 yards deep, but only 9ft diameter) here employed 729 men underground and 133 above, and not surprisingly worked the Rowhurst coal. The No.2 shaft, the principal coal winder, had cages with three decks and could take six tubs with a total capacity of three tons per wind. The No.1 pit, though it also had cages with three decks, was of smaller size so could only raise 25 cwts per wind. There were seven Lancashire boilers to provide steam for the winding, ventilation, pumping and some underground haulage engines. Notice the dumb buffered wagons. The pits here closed in 1908, when major surface developments at nearby Hanley Deep Pit Colliery, also owned by the company, came on stream and the underground workings were connected. The Rowhurst pits were always known locally as Slippery Lane Colliery. (Map 7)

The Hall Pit was so named as it was alongside Etruria Hall, built by Josiah Wedgwood for his family. The hall was later engulfed within the iron and steel works, becoming its main offices. Here is the Hall Pit in 1891, with Etruria Hall beyond. This pit was 345 yards deep and 13ft diameter, but coal was not wound here, the shaft being used for men, materials, pumping and ventilation. Water was drawn not only by the winding engine with water filled tubs, but also by a 'Bull' type 'Cornish' cycle beam pumping engine and a pair of bucket lifts – steam was generated by a battery of six cylindrical egg-ended boilers working at 60 psi. Notice the wagons delivering coal for the boilers, and the narrow gauge railway in the left foreground. (Map 7)

The blast furnaces at Shelton on 1 September 1916, with work underway in the foreground to construct a hot metal mixer. Much improvement work was done at Shelton during the early part of the First World War with financial assistance from the Government to increase production. This included new steel making plant, a new blast furnace, high level bunkers and mechanical charging for all the furnaces. From left to right can be seen the slag banks (the chimneys in distance mark the site of the Grange Colliery, Burslem), blowing engine house and blast furnaces. In the foreground, in front of the furnaces, can be seen the piles of pigs and one of the Andrew Barclay 0-4-0 saddle tank shunting engines engaged in moving slag from the furnaces to the tips. There were several of these locomotives at Shelton, dating from the turn of the century. (Map 7)

Two views taken in 1891 of the Racecourse Colliery, built on the site of an old racecourse. The first shows the No.5 pit, 150 yards deep and 9½ft in diameter, at this time used for drawing ironstone. There were 175 men employed underground and 57 above. Notice the exposed winding engine, narrow gauge tubs and standard gauge wagons marked EG – for Earl Granville – and S.I.S&C Co – Shelton Iron Steel & Coal Company. The second view shows the No.3 pit, 330 yards deep and 13½ft in diameter which drew coal and ironstone and employed at this time 338 men underground and 167 above. There was a further pit here, No.4 which was the upcast and had a 40ft diameter 'Guibal' fan for ventilation purposes – steam was supplied for all three pits by a battery of fourteen egg-ended boilers working at 60 psi, similar to those at the Hall Pit. Notice again the narrow gauge tubs, horses for hauling them and the loading chute to left. The Racecourse pits were situated north-west of the main iron and steel works site, west of the Cobridge Road and were much modernised over the years. During the early part of the Second World War they were drawing ironstone, but closure came in 1941 when this mineral was completely worked out so far as economic operations were concerned. The site was later used as a coal and coke stocking ground, and after closure of the iron and steel-making plant was occupied by part of the 1986 Stoke-on-Trent Garden Festival; currently it is the site of a retail park. (Map 7)

Two views taken from Bradwell Woods looking east across the ex-NSR main line at the Shelton Iron & Steel Works, at two different dates. The first dates from 1959 and in the background from left to right can be seen the blast furnaces and charging hoists and the four parallel steel symmetrical chimneys of the steel melting shop, followed by the slag reduction plant. Curving away out of the picture is the works railway line connecting the Etruria Yard sidings with the main works site. The pottery bottle ovens mark the site of the Wedgwood pottery manufactory. In front of the works and obscuring much of it is the slag bank, representing many years of slag tipping from the days when little or no use could be found for this by-product of the iron smelting process. The ex-NSR main line runs across the picture, with Etruria Yard and its signal box on the Up side (top), and Grange Yard on the down side (bottom); notice the ex-LMS 3F 0-6-0 shunting tank busy at work. The second view dates from 1978 and is the scene further north, the two photographs almost abutting each other. The blast furnaces and charging hoists again form the centre piece, with the long building to the right being the old steel melting shop – behind and above it can be seen Etruria Hall. By this time steel production was in the hands of two 45-ton Kaldo converters, which employed the Oxygen principle of steel making. Commissioned in June 1964, they were capable of making a cast of steel in 45 minutes. This 'new' steel making plant was situated off the picture to the left. The slag bank by this time has almost completely disappeared, largely utilised as hardcore for motorway construction. By this time the slag was recovered almost as soon as it was tipped. In the foreground is the ex-NSR main line, Kidsgrove to the left and Stoke to the right, with the modern 'BR' style Grange Junction signal box and Wolstanton Colliery sidings. The overhead covered box section trunking carried a conveyer so that coal from this colliery could be transported directly to the iron and steel works for coking. When the coking plant closed at Shelton in May 1968, however, coke came from the John Summers works at Shotton near Chester. Some Wolstanton coal was still loaded by this conveyer system for onward transport by rail to Shotton for coking, and then came back again for use in the blast furnaces – what price progress? (Map 7) Photographs E.J.D. Warrillow, Keele University Library and Allan C. Baker.

The towpath of the Trent and Mersey Canal in 1950 looking west; the canal ran right through the middle of the iron and steel works. Part of the coking plant can be seen here, with the cylindrical coal washer building to the left, a battery of coke ovens in the centre, and the coal bunkers to the right. At this time the coking plant here, with its several separate batteries of ovens, was capable of producing around 550,000 tons of coke per annum, most of which was consumed on site. Gas from the ovens was used not only for firing the blast furnaces and ancillary plant, but the steel furnaces too, and from 1935 surplus gas was sold to the local authority for domestic and industrial consumption. In 1953 a further battery of twenty-four by-product recovery ovens were added to the plant. The row of private owner wagons include two five plank ones used for internal operations only – known to the men as 'EGs', for Earl Granville. The narrow boat OUSE belonging to J. Colclough appears to have a cargo of coal, and one of the boatmen's push bikes can be seen in the hold – this is a horse drawn boat. (Map 7) Photograph E.J.D. Warrillow, Keele University Library.

Photograph taken in March 1941 looking north along the Trent and Mersey Canal, with the bridge taking the NSR Potteries Loop Line and the Shelton internal railway across it. The building on the left is the 32in steel rolling mill ('32in' refers to the 'working' section of the rolls); then, from left to right, come the coking oven plant, by-product chemical works and Etruria Hall with the Racecourse Colliery dirt tip behind. Notice how wide the canal is hereabouts, as it used to go under the railway further to the left, having been diverted as a part of the scheme to introduce passenger traffic on the line to Hanley, so as to reduce the gradient of the railway. The steel works Hudswell Clarke 0-6-0 side tank shunting locomotive is hauling a train from the exchange sidings at Etruria – this is PEPLOW, maker's number 1707 of 1939. PEPLOW took its name from Peplow Hall near Hodnet in Shropshire, home of one of the Shelton Directors, Neville H. Rollason. In the foreground is a part of the Wedgwood Pottery, which had originally been at the same level as the canal, but mining subsidence over the years has taken its toll. (Map 7) Photograph E.J.D. Warrillow, Keele University Library.

Slag from the old Shelton (Cobridge Road) furnaces (they were situated to the extreme right centre in this picture) was deposited at Tinkersclough, and this view looking north-west on August Bank Holiday Monday 1949, is from the top of the old tip. To be seen from left to right are the steel rolling mill buildings, blast furnaces, coking plant and chemical works, rear of Etruria Hall followed by the gasholders and power station. Extreme right is the Racecourse Colliery dirt tip with part of the village of Etruria in the foreground; the tall building to right centre alongside the Loop Line Railway bridge is the Rose & Crown pub – just about the only building in this scene still standing today! Notice the Loop Line curving its way through the photograph, with Wolstanton Church providing a landmark on the horizon. (Map 7) Photograph E.J.D. Warrillow, Keele University Library.

A rather poor, but nevertheless very interesting, 1943 aerial view of the Shelton iron and steel works looking north-west. Across the bottom can be seen the Potteries Loop Line and the Trent and Mersey Canal – the canal used to run right through what in this view is the 32in rolling mill building. It was diverted to the right to allow easing of the Loop Line railway gradient. The blast furnaces are above the mill, with the coke ovens and by-product plant in the centre and Etruria Hall to extreme centre right. To the top right can just be seen the Grange railway exchange sidings and iron ore preparation plant. (Map 7) Photograph E.J.D. Warrillow, Keele University Library.

GLENALMOND, a 14in cylinder 0-4-0 saddle tank shunting locomotive built at the Shelton works in 1912. However well equipped the workshops were to repair and rebuild locomotives, actually building one complete was no mean achievement, and no less than four were completed at Shelton over the years. The pattern for this one and indeed one other is clearly that of Scottish builder Andrew Barclay Sons & Company Limited, a Kilmarnock firm which supplied a number of locomotives for use at the works over the years. GLENALMOND here is brand new and just out of the workshops, doubtless undergoing its first steam trials – she was named after the Scottish Estate near Perth of Lord Faringdon, Chairman of the company at the time, and lasted until 1972. Most unfortunately in view of its parentage, it was not saved for preservation, despite some efforts on my part. Notice the addition of a copper capped chimney; none of her stable mates boasted such an adornment. Management and men were always very proud of this locomotive at Shelton, affectionately known to one and all as 'Glenny', and when almost all the other engines had to make do with a coat of black paint, GLENALMOND retained a nice green livery and was always kept clean! (Map 7) Photograph Collection Basil Jeuda.

HOLMBURY, one of the Kilmarnock-built four wheelers, Andrew Barclay maker's number 860 of 1900, seen here on 2 March 1957 alongside the blast furnaces – there is a furnace slag ladle wagon in the left background. There were no less than eight locomotives of this general type used at Shelton in 'steam' days, always collectively known as 'Kilmarnocks'. HOLMBURY took her name from Holmbury St Mary in Surrey, home of the son of the First Earl Granville, Lord Leveson (and the Second Earl); it lasted until cut up for scrap in 1972. (Map 7) Photograph Industrial Railway Society, Bernard Mettam Collection.

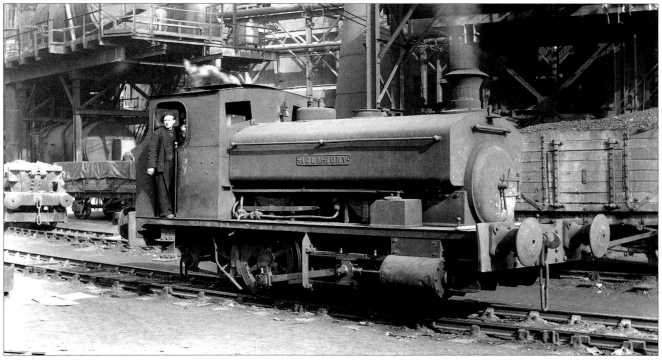

One of the larger works shunting locomotives was LORD FARINGDON (named after Sir Alexander Henderson, Chairman at the time) acquired from the Darlington dealer John F. Wake about 1915. Black Hawthorn & Company of Gateshead-on-Tyne (maker's number 242) built this locomotive in 1873 for the North Eastern Railway, where it became its No.868 of Class 964. It was renumbered 1746 in October 1888 and rebuilt as Class 964A in 1893 when it reverted to its original number. Withdrawn in April 1911, it was purchased by Wake, repaired and sold to Shelton. LORD FARINGDON lasted until diesels started to arrive at the works and was scrapped in 1955; this is the locomotive in the mid-1930s shunting on the Racecourse, as the coal stocking ground was called, adjacent to the site of the colliery of that name. This was alongside the Cobridge Road between Etruria and Cobridge itself. (Map 7) Photograph Industrial Railway Society, H.W. Robinson Collection.

Tipping the slag at Shelton on 7 May 1969, with HAWARDEN, built locally by W.G. Bagnall Limited of Stafford in 1940 – maker's number 2623. This was the last new steam locomotive delivered to Shelton, and the last in use; withdrawn in the early months of 1972 it was saved for preservation and is currently in regular use on the nearby Foxfield Light Railway at Blythe Bridge. HAWARDEN took its name from the Hawarden Bridge Steel Works at Shotton, near Chester, of John Summers & Sons Limited, the parent Company of Shelton at the time. The locomotive has moved away from the slag ladle wagon before it was tipped – this was done using the chain, attached to the loco's draw hook. The wagons in the foreground, despite the wording on one of them, are loaded with coal prior to being taken to the John Summers plant at Shotton where the coal would be coked. They will have been loaded with coal from Wolstanton Colliery via the overhead conveyor. (Map 7) Photograph Allan C. Baker.

Two views of the blast furnace plant at Shelton, taken from the Trent and Mersey Canal on 24 March 1978. Notice the distinctive charging hoists, hot blast stoves, high-level railway to feed the coke, ore and limestone bunkers, and the piles of scrap. This was almost at the end of the life of this plant, as iron and steel making ceased at Shelton in June 1978. (Map 7) Photographs Allan C. Baker.

The 'Bogie Hole' as it was known, where the blast furnaces were tapped for both the slag and the iron before transport to the slag bank and steel plant respectively. This view shows the slag and metal ladle wagons, with the No.6 blast furnaces above – 26 May 1978. (Map 7) Photograph Allan C. Baker.

Tapping the No.6 blast furnace at Shelton on 26 May 1978, just a few weeks before iron production ceased at the works. The molten iron has just started to flow down towards one of the rail mounted ladles seen in the previous photograph. On the right a second runway is already prepared for the molten metal; this one will be used once the ladle wagon currently catching the metal flow is full, the molten metal being diverted via this second runway to another waiting ladle wagon. (Map 7) Photograph Allan C. Baker.

One of the four steam turbine driven blowers for the blast furnaces at Shelton, blowers of this type having replaced the reciprocating beam engines in the First World War modernisation. The English Electric Company Limited built this one in 1920 at its Ordnance Works in Coventry. When this photograph was taken on 26 May 1978, just a few weeks before iron production ceased at Shelton, it was running together with another, for two blowers were needed for the two blast furnaces then in operation. There were three furnaces in total, and if all three were in blast, three blowers were necessary, leaving one spare. The No.1 furnace had a hearth diameter of 17ft 6in, No.4 10ft 6in and No.6 12ft 9in. Furnace Nos.2, 3 and 5 had been dismantled many years earlier, but the numbering sequence had been retained. At the time of closure of the iron works Nos.4 and 6 blast furnaces were in blast, and No.1 was never 'blown' again after this picture was taken. Visitors were not normally allowed around this part of the works (and photography was completely forbidden!) but a friendship with the then General Manager, Derek Field, resulted in permission being granted to a limited number of interested folk, in view of the impending closure of the iron and steel producing part of the plant. After closure only the rolling mill was retained, and billets from other British Steel plants were brought to Shelton by rail, re-heated and rolled into various different sections prior to sale – it was a very efficient mill hence its retention. However, this too eventually came to an end, and production ceased on 27 April 2000. (Map 7) Photograph Allan C. Baker.

An interesting locomotive employed at Shelton from 1901 until 1970 was this six ton capacity crane tank, built by Dubs of Glasgow (maker's number 4101) seen here busy helping to re-rail a wagon in the late 1960s. By this time (1961) the engine had been converted to burn oil fuel – the oil tank is underneath the crane balance weight. This conversion was to enable the engine to quickly raise steam if its crane capabilities were needed in a hurry because of some incident around the works when it was not otherwise in use. Withdrawn in 1970, it went into preservation with the Cranmore Railway in Somerset. It left Shelton in September 1973 but returned to North Staffordshire a couple of years ago, and has joined its old stable mate HAWARDEN on the Foxfield Light Railway at Blythe Bridge. However, it has not yet been restored to working order. (Map 7) Photograph Dave Donkin.

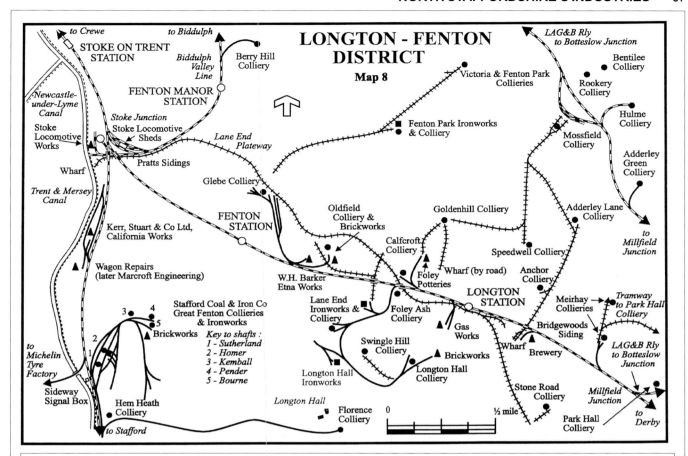

LONGTON - FENTON DISTRICT

Map 8

to Crewe
to Biddulph
LAG&B Rly to Botteslow Junction
STOKE ON TRENT STATION
Biddulph Valley Line
Berry Hill Colliery
Bentilee Colliery
Rookery Colliery
Victoria & Fenton Park Collieries
FENTON MANOR STATION
Newcastle-under-Lyme Canal
Stoke Junction
Stoke Locomotive Sheds
Lane End Plateway
Fenton Park Ironworks & Colliery
Hulme Colliery
Mossfield Colliery
Adderley Green Colliery
Stoke Locomotive Works
Pratts Sidings
Wharf
Trent & Mersey Canal
Glebe Colliery
FENTON STATION
Oldfield Colliery & Brickworks
Goldenhill Colliery
Adderley Lane Colliery
to Millfield Junction
Kerr, Stuart & Co Ltd, California Works
Calfcroft Colliery
Speedwell Colliery
Wagon Repairs (later Marcroft Engineering)
W.H. Barker Etna Works
Foley Potteries
Wharf (by road)
Anchor Colliery
Meirhay Collieries
Tramway to Park Hall Colliery
Stafford Coal & Iron Co Great Fenton Collieries & Ironworks
Brickworks
Key to shafts :
1 - Sutherland
2 - Homer
3 - Kemball
4 - Pender
5 - Bourne
Lane End Ironworks & Colliery
Foley Ash Colliery
LONGTON STATION
Bridgewoods Siding
LAG&B Rly to Botteslow Junction
to Michelin Tyre Factory
Swingle Hill Colliery
Gas Works
Wharf
Brewery
Sideway Signal Box
Hem Heath Colliery
Brickworks
Longton Hall Ironworks
Longton Hall Colliery
Stone Road Colliery
Millfield Junction
to Derby
to Stafford
Longton Hall
Florence Colliery
0   ½ mile
Park Hall Colliery

Hanley Deep Pit in 1932 looking south-east. So named because it became the deepest of the pits on or near the iron and steelworks site, in its heyday it had one of the deepest shafts in the North Staffordshire coalfield. Originally sunk in 1854 by Earl Granville to serve the needs of his iron works at Shelton, it was to remain in the ownership of the iron and steel works until nationalisation of the coal industry on 1 January 1947. This pit was extensively developed so that by 1908, apart from Racecourse, all the other pits on the main iron and steelworks site, or adjacent to it, were closed and the workings connected underground to the Deep Pit. In 1898-89, a private mineral railway had been built by the Shelton Company to connect this pit directly with the main works. It remained in use to serve the works' needs even after the colliery ceased to be owed by the Shelton Company, until the colliery closed in 1962 in fact. In 1930, the Deep Pit employed 1,552 men underground and 395 above, and in 1936 drew no less than 660,000 tons of coal, although this was a peak year and figures around the 400,000 tons mark were more the norm. In this view we can see to the left the No.2 downcast shaft (the coal winder) and to the right the No.1 upcast shaft – both were sunk to a depth of 850 yards. (Map 7) Photograph William Jack.

Another view of the Deep Pit, this time in the early 1950s and looking in exactly the opposite direction to the previous view, with the No.1 upcast shaft to the left and the No.2 downcast to the right – notice the air lock on the former headgear. In 1947 this pit drew 350,114 tons of coal with 1,285 men, but by 1960 production was down to 252,036 tons with 1,000 men. Developments at Wolstanton Colliery were partly designed to supersede operations here, by connecting the workings underground and the pit closed in May 1962. (Map 7) Photograph E.J.D. Warrillow, Keele University Library.

New Ubberley Colliery at Bucknall, part of the Chatterley Whitfield Colliery Empire – one of its wagons is in the foreground. The pit was sunk in the period 1874-75, to the Cockshead coal seam at a depth of 420 yards. There were several other pits hereabouts, all acquired by the Chatterley Iron Company Limited (predecessor of Chatterley Whitfield Collieries Limited) but they never quite lived up to expectations, such that when New Ubberley closed in November 1904, it was the last one operating. This picture appears to have been taken after closure, as there is little activity apparent, and the surface operations are beginning to look rather decrepit. Notice the tall winding engine house, which had a vertical winding engine thought to have been built by a relatively local builder, Scragg of Congleton in Cheshire. Notice too, the second pit headgear behind (Map 9) Photograph Collection William Jack.